# A Day with the Animals on

# Upland Hills Farm

Nathan Perkins
**"Farmer Nate"**

Morning comes early at Upland Hills Farm. Farmer Leslie's grandchildren Cooper, Ryan, Bella, Sydney, and Sawyer are going to help her do the chores. She is putting on her boots because it is time to bring the cows in for milking.

Farmer Steve has a lot of work to do. He waves good morning to his grandchildren before he climbs on the tractor.

This cow's name is Fern. Farmer Leslie is showing her grandchildren how to milk the cow by hand. She accidentally squirts herself with milk and the children laugh.

We call animals that give us milk dairy animals. Fern is a dairy cow. We call foods that we make from milk dairy products. Farmer Leslie uses milk to make a lot of different dairy products like cheese, butter, and ice cream.

"Eddee, don't drink the milk!"

Farmer Leslie's dog, Eddee, is trying to sneak a drink of milk from the bucket.

Farmer Leslie uses some of the milk she gets from the cow to feed the baby cows. We call a baby cow a calf. Bella is having fun feeding the calf.

Cows are not the only dairy animals on the farm. Goats can also give us milk. People all over the world use goat milk to drink and to make dairy products.

We call a mother goat a nanny goat. This is a nanny goat and her baby. Did you know that girl goats have horns? When an animal has horns both the boys and girls will grow horns.

Do you see the kid in this picture?

Sometimes we call human children kids.
We also call baby goats kids.

We call the father goat a billy goat.

Whose funny face is this?  She has pink
skin, wiry hair and a round nose.

Can you see the milk on the animal's chin?  Farmer Leslie just
gave this baby pig a bottle. We call a baby pig a piglet.

Some people keep pigs as pets.  Do you think
that a pig would make a good pet?

There are two reasons why a pig might make a good
pet.  The first reason is that they are very smart.  The
other reason is that pigs are one of the cleanest
animals on the farm.  Does that surprise you?

Pigs take baths.  Sure, it looks messy and dirty when they roll in the mud, but the mud works like soap and cleans the pig's skin.  Also, if you had a pig in your house, you could teach it to use a litter box like a cat.

This pig would not make a good pet.  It will get too big.  Pigs like this one weigh 350 pounds before they are one year old.

Farmer Leslie is showing the children a piglet. When Farmer Leslie picks it up, the piglet squeals. The children cover their ears because it is so loud. Farmer Leslie tells the children the piglet is going to be a good singer someday. The children all laugh.

Why does the piglet really squeal?

Maybe the piglet is hungry. Sometimes piglets squeal because, like human babies, they want a bottle when they get hungry.

Farmer Leslie asks the children if they are ready to get some eggs. Where will they go to get the eggs?

You are right when you say eggs come from a grocery store. But where does a grocery store get eggs from? A grocery store gets eggs from chickens on a farm.

Farmer Leslie and her grandchildren collect the eggs.  Some of the eggs are brown and some are green.  These eggs are not white like the ones you see at the grocery store.

The children know that they can eat brown and green eggs.

Sawyer asks his grandma if there will be any baby chicks inside these eggs.  He knows a baby chicken is called a chick.

Farmer Leslie smiles because she has a secret.

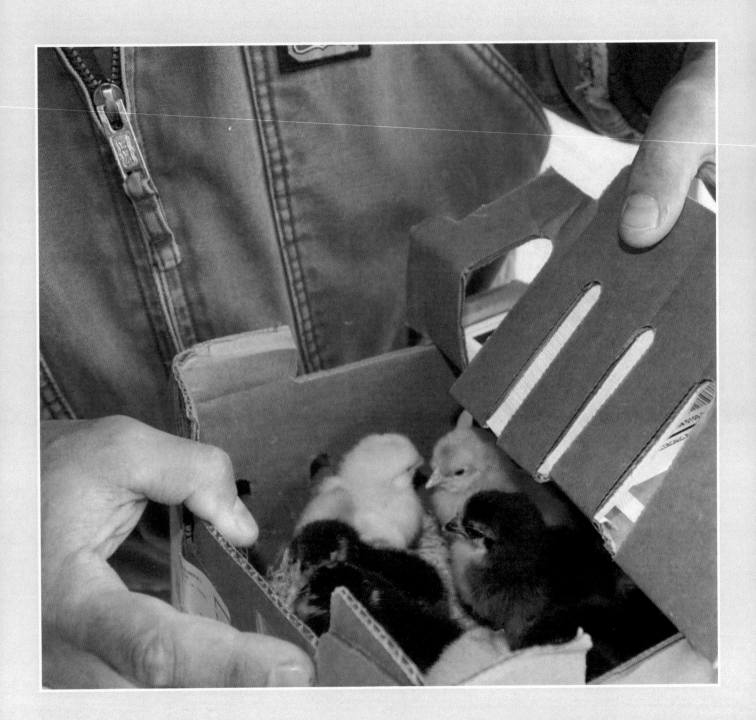

Farmer Steve says, "I've got something for you."
He is carrying a strange looking box.

The children want to know what is making
the chirping sound inside the box.

Farmer Steve opens the box and shows the children what he just
picked up at the post office.  There are baby chicks in the box.

Sometimes chicks are born on the farm.  Other
times Farmer Steve orders them from another
farmer, who sends them in the mail.

The children and Farmer Leslie put the chicks
in a brooder.  The brooder is a small box with
a light in it that keeps the chicks warm.

We call the female chicken a hen. Mother hen sits on her eggs to keep them warm. She will have to sit on her eggs for 21 days for chicks to grow inside the eggs. When a chick is fully grown it will use its beak to break the shell. We call that hatching.

What do we call the father chicken?

The father chicken is called a rooster.

You can see that the rooster has a big red comb on the top of his head and large wattles under his chin. That is how we know this is a rooster. A hen's comb and wattles are smaller. The rooster also grows a long nail on the back of his leg called a spur.

Does the rooster have a job on the farm?

The rooster's job is to make a big sound. We call that sound the rooster's crow. When the rooster crows he sometimes wakes up the farmer. But he is not trying to wake up the farmer. The rooster crows all day long because that is his way of talking to the other chickens.

Can you make the sound a rooster makes?

We call the birds on the farm poultry animals. Poultry animals give the farmer both meat and eggs.

Upland Hills Farm has a lot of ducks. Farmer Steve is feeding the ducks cracked corn.

It is hard to tell a girl duck from a boy duck but Farmer Leslie is showing her grandchildren the secret. Take a look at the duck's tail. The boy duck grows a curled feather.

Sometimes the boy duck will lose its curled feather. Then how can we tell the difference?

One duck has a louder voice then the other. Do you think the boy duck or girl duck has the louder voice?

The girl duck is louder. She will use her loud voice to protect her babies by calling them to safety on the pond.

We call a baby duck a duckling. Farmer Leslie shows
her grandchildren the ducklings. These ducklings
will turn white when they get their adult feathers.
Do you see the puff of feathers on the duckling's
heads? They look like they have silly hair.

Geese are the only animals on the farm that pick a mate for life. That is like getting married. They spend all their time together.

In some countries, people give a pair of geese as a wedding gift to wish the couple good luck.

Do you think a pair of geese would be a funny gift?

The baby goose is called a gosling. The mother is called the goose. The father goose is called the gander.

Geese make a sound like a car horn. If a pair of geese get separated, one goose will honk and the other one will respond back until they find each other again.

Farmer Steve is shearing the sheep. Every year the sheep will grow a thick coat. The coat is made of wool and is very warm. When Farmer Steve shears the sheep, he gets some wool that can be used to make many different things.

Look how dirty the sheep's coat is!

After Farmer Steve shears a sheep, Farmer Leslie does several things to the wool to get it ready for knitting.

First she washes the wool. Then she teases the wool. To tease the wool she pulls it apart over and over. Teasing the wool causes the dirt and grass to fall to the ground.

Now the wool is clean but it is still full of knots and snarls. To get the snarls out, Farmer Leslie will brush the wool with special brushes called carders.

Farmer Leslie can't knit a pair of gloves yet. The wool keeps falling apart. Before Farmer Leslie makes anything out of the wool, she will turn it into yarn. She does this by twisting the fibers in the wool together using a drop spinner or a spinning wheel. When she spins the drop spinner, the wool twists into yarn. As she adds more wool the yarn gets longer. Then she will wrap the yarn onto the spinner.

A spinning wheel is faster
because it wraps the yarn onto
the spool while Farmer Leslie
is spinning it. She can keep
making yarn until she runs out
of wool or until her spool is full.

Now she has a lot of yarn and
she can make gloves, socks,
a scarf or a hat. She could
even make a sweater.

Her grandchildren each
ask, "Grandma, what are
you making for me?"

Finally, all of the day's work is done at Upland Hills Farm and the sun sets. Farmers Steve and Leslie will wake up early again tomorrow to take care of the animals.

# Biographies

### Farmers Steve and Leslie Webster

*Farmer Steve's parents, Knight and Dorothy Webster, started Upland Hills Farm in the Detroit area in 1960 with the idea that it would bring the joys and lessons of rural life to an ever increasing urban society. Steve and Leslie met at Upland Hills Farm when Leslie came to work as a camp counselor. They married in 1971 and now run the farm together, maintaining the drive and vision that springs from the lessons they learned on the farm. They work to pass those lessons on to campers, visitors, their own children and grandchildren. Their grandchildren, Ryan, Sydney, Bella, Cooper, and Sawyer are pictured in this book.*

### Author Farmer Nate Perkins

*Farmer Nate shares a passion for both education and agriculture. He presents shows for the over 100,000 people who visit Upland Hills Farm each year. During the summer he is one of the directors at Upland Hills Farm Day Camp. He also writes fiction to bring people visions of hope. He has completed several fiction and nonfiction books and is seeking their publication.*

*Nathan, his wife Pam and their sons live just a few miles from the farm in Leonard, Michigan.*

### Farmer Caleb Perkins

*Farmer Caleb has worked at Upland Hills Farm since he was 13 years old. During the summer he is a camp counselor at Upland Hills Farm Day Camp and in the spring and fall he gives tours to children who come to the farm on school fieldtrips. The farm has been a great place to practice the art of photography.*

*Farmer Caleb will start attending Cornerstone University just shortly after the publication of this book. He has entered with a declared major of Photojournalism.*

WestBow Press books may be ordered through booksellers or by contacting:

WestBow Press
A Division of Thomas Nelson
1663 Liberty Drive
Bloomington, IN 47403
www.westbowpress.com
1-(866) 928-1240

Because of the dynamic nature of the Internet, any web addresses or links contained in
this book may have changed since publication and may no longer be valid. The views
expressed in this work are solely those of the author and do not necessarily reflect the views
of the publisher, and the publisher hereby disclaims any responsibility for them.

Any people depicted in stock imagery provided by Thinkstock are models,
and such images are being used for illustrative purposes only.

Certain stock imagery © Thinkstock.

ISBN: 978-1-4497-3791-7 (sc)

Library of Congress Control Number: 2012901468

Printed in the United States of America

WestBow Press rev. date: 2/24/2012

WestBow
PRESS
A DIVISION OF THOMAS NELSON

Made in the USA
Lexington, KY
31 August 2012